Tools for Teaching

ALMA HEATON

Illustrated by Richard Holdaway

Bookcraft
Salt Lake City, Utah

Copyright © 1979 by Bookcraft, Inc.
All rights reserved

Library of Congress Catalog Card Number: 79-53129
ISBN O-88494-379-8

7 8 9 10   89 88 87 86 85

Lithographed in the United States of America
PUBLISHERS PRESS
Salt Lake City, Utah

PREFACE

Are your church or family home evening lessons producing the desired results? Do your students or family members spend valuable time just watching or listening as the lesson is given, or does each one actively participate?

One of the greatest challenges a teacher faces is to build within the student an interest in learning. One way to motivate interest is to use an unusual and striking way to teach. Teaching tools are an effective means of quieting students as they enter the classroom and of quickly focusing their attention on the subject matter. These tools can also be used for reference later on in the lesson.

This book, *Tools for Teaching*, can provide meaningful sources of information and a wide variety of learning experiences. A teaching tool thoroughly mastered can extend the horizon of a child's experience and provide a fresh, interesting way of learning the gospel.

Not only do we need to be happy ourselves, but we should help make others happy. If a teacher's methods evoke happiness and a sense of fun which assists the learning process, the teacher is fulfilling his calling in helping class members learn and keep our Father's commandments.

CONTENTS

Activity in the Church	1
Adversity	2
Appearance	3
Appearance	4
Application of the Gospel	5
Balance	6
Blessings	7
Charity	8
Choice	9
Creation of Man	10
Death	11
Deception	12
Enduring to the End	13
Enthusiasm	14
Faith	15
Faith and Works	16
Family Love	17
Forgiving Ourselves	18
Goals	19
Gospel	20
Gospel Enrichment	21
Hardships	22
Heart of Gold	23
Light	24
Marriage	25
Moral Cleanliness	26
Obstacles	27
Our Bodies	28
Overcoming Problems	29

Contents

Prayer	30
Prayer	31
Priesthood	32
Principles of the Gospel	33
Principles and Ordinances of the Gospel	34
Priorities	35
Procrastination	36
Protection	37
Purpose in Life	38
Readiness	39
Repentance	40
Satan	41
Self-Esteem	42
Service	43
Sin	44
Speaking Kind Words	45
Spirituality	46
Strong Physical Body	47
Talents	48
Talents	49
Testimony	50
Testimony	51
Time	52
Trust	53
Trust	54
Unity	55
Use of Time	56
Well-Rounded Person	57
The Whole Armor of God	58

ACTIVITY IN THE CHURCH

Objective: To show that when we cease to be active we cease to learn and progress.

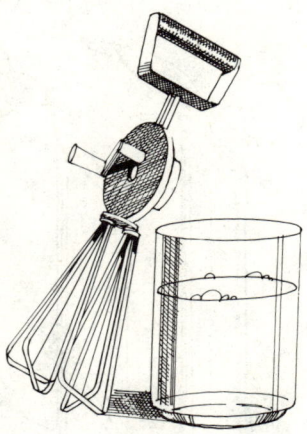

Material Needed:

1. Egg beater
2. A liquid, such as whipping cream, that will show the effects of being beaten

Presentation:

1. Turn the beater in the air.
2. Turn the beater in the liquid.

Lesson Application:

1. The beater is not worth much unless you use its working parts to help you out. If you just turn the handle in midair, all you are going to do is stir up a little air. But if you put the beater in a liquid and turn the handle you will get results. The faster you turn the handle, the faster you get results.
2. Your life is worthless unless you take advantage of what you have.
3. If you do not do anything with the gospel, you will receive no results.
4. If you allow the gospel to be a part of your life, you will begin to grow and get results from the Lord. The more effort you put into living the gospel, the more results you will receive.

Tools for Teaching

ADVERSITY

Objective: To show how we are tested by adversity.

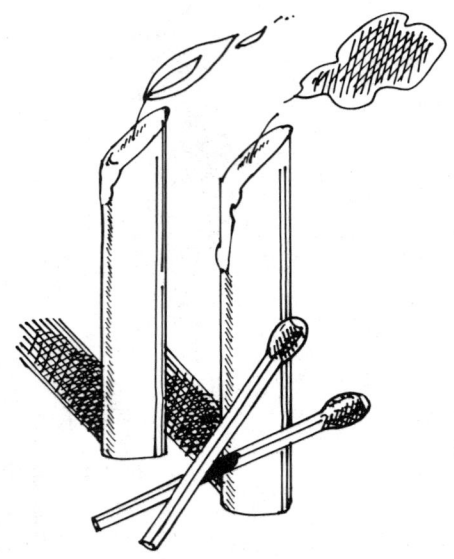

Material Needed:

1. Two candles (One must be a trick candle that relights)
2. Matches

Presentation:

1. Light both candles.
2. Let them burn for a moment while explaining that both candles look alike.
3. Then blow out both candles. (One candle will go out but the other will relight.)

Lesson Application:

1. Each candle represents a person on this earth.
2. The candle that went out represents the man who cannot handle adversity—he gets discouraged and his light goes out and can no longer shine to the world.
3. The candle that did not go out represents the man who overcomes adversity and thus lets his light shine to all the world.

APPEARANCE

Objective: To show that appearances can be deceiving.

Material Needed:

1. Sugar cookies frosted with different frostings (Some frostings should contain salt as well as sugar)

Presentation:

1. On a plate in view of class members, arrange the cookies. (The cookies should look appetizing.) Members of the class should be encouraged to nibble on the cookies.
2. Soon someone will discover the salty frosting. Ask him to describe the difference between what he was expecting and what he got.

Lesson Application:

1. Something that appears to be sweet might not be good at all.
2. Sweet things can hide under a salty covering. Look for inner strength and beauty.

APPEARANCE

Objective: To show that we should not judge by appearance alone.

Material Needed:

1. Two pens, one that works and one that does not (The one that does not work should be the more attractive pen)

Presentation:

1. Have someone examine the pens without using them.
2. Have him decide—from appearance—which is the better pen.
3. Have someone use each pen.
4. Ask which is the better pen for writing.

Lesson Application:

1. We are all created with divine spiritual potential, but some of us never fill our lives with the experiences and work necessary to make us useful.
2. Sometimes people appear to be good but are actually bad.
3. All that some people need is others to fill their emptiness with gospel experiences and love.

APPLICATION OF THE GOSPEL

Objective: To show that we must apply the gospel to our lives in order to fulfill our potential.

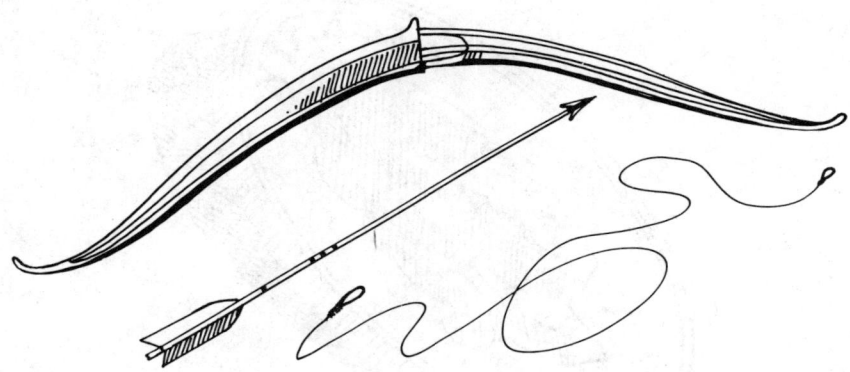

Material Needed:

1. Bow and string
2. Arrow

Presentation:

1. Have a student try to make use of the bow without the string.
2. Explain that while we may discover other uses for the bow, without the string it cannot fulfill its true purpose. The arrow will have no direction.

Lesson Application:

1. Without the gospel in our lives, we will have no direction, and we will not be able to fulfill the purpose of our existence.

BALANCE

Objective: To show that we must concentrate on achieving balance in our lives.

Material Needed:

1. A coin (One large enough to be seen by the entire class)

Presentation:

1. Before class, practice balancing the coin on its side.
2. Quickly place the coin on its side and let it fall over.
3. Now concentrate and slowly balance the coin on its side.
4. Hit the table so that the coin falls over. Once again concentrate and slowly place the coin on its side.

Lesson Application:

1. Our lives are like the coin—if we don't concentrate on having balance in our lives (a variety of activities) we will fall over, so to speak. But if we do concentrate and work, slowly but surely we will achieve this balance.
2. We might receive knocks that cause us to lose balance, but once we have learned to concentrate we can regain that balance.

BLESSINGS

Objective: To show the importance of a thankful heart.

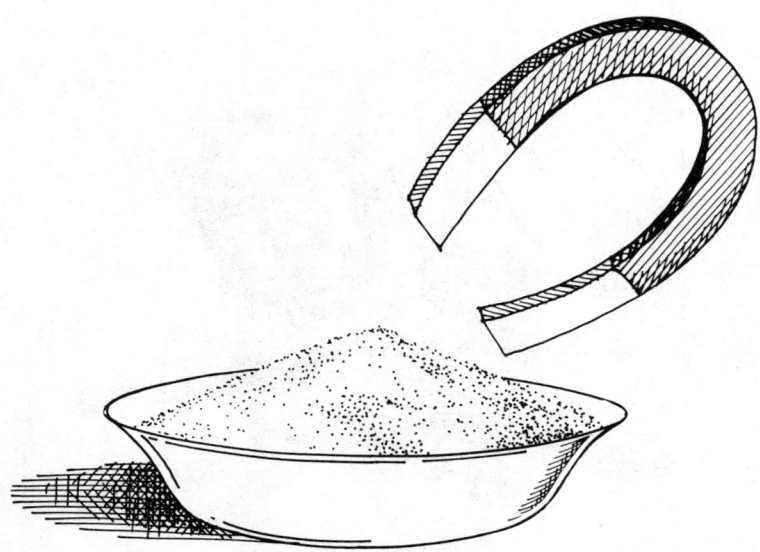

Material Needed:
1. Small dish of sand with iron filings in it
2. Magnet

Presentation:
1. Tell a student there are particles of iron in the sand and ask him to find them. He will probably express some negative reaction to the assignment.
2. Then ask another student to do the same thing but give him a magnet.
3. Direct discussion so that the class understands you analogy: both students had the same dish (or portion in life), but one used the magnet (a thankful heart) to find value in a seemingly useless pile of sand.

Lesson Application:
1. The Lord has given us many blessings. We can increase our awareness of those blessings if we have thankful hearts.
2. We can find some good in everyone.
3. We frequently find what we look for.

8　Tools for Teaching

CHARITY

Objective: To show what Jesus meant when he spoke of "the least of these my brethren."

Material Needed:

1. Darts
2. Picture of an unpopular figure
3. Picture of Jesus Christ

Presentation:

1. Place the picture of the unpopular figure on a bulletin board and pass out the darts. See who can hit the picture.
2. Place the picture of the Savior on the bulletin board and ask who wants to throw darts at this picture. Notice the reactions of the students. Comment.

Lesson Application:

1. Jesus said, "Inasmuch as ye have done it unto one of the least of these my brethren, ye have done it unto me." (Matthew 25:40.)
2. The Lord wants us to be kind to all men, just as we would be kind to him. Although we may at first want to harm people who are unkind to us, we should remember that the way of the world is retaliation and the way of Christ is forgiveness.
3. Discuss the following statement by Abraham Lincoln: "Am I not destroying my enemies when I make them my friends?"

Tools for Teaching

CHOICE

Objective: To show that we need to make decisions with eternal consequences in mind.

Material Needed:

1. A ripe, juicy orange
2. A candy bar

Presentation:

1. After showing the students the orange and the candy bar, ask them which of the two they would like to have.
2. Next ask them why they have chosen what they have.
3. Now, give each student a piece of the candy bar or orange, depending on his choice.

Lesson Application:

1. First speak to those who chose the candy bar: You have chosen the food that will give you quick energy. It is very sweet and pleasing to eat. However, it is not long-lasting and sometimes leaves a bitter aftertaste in your mouth. It is mostly empty calories.
2. Now speak to those who chose the orange: The orange also will give you energy and is sweet to the taste. However, the orange has more nutritional value and will supply you with vitamin C. Yours was a wise decision.
3. This can be compared to the decisions we make in life. We can either choose those things which bring us immediate pleasure but have no long-lasting value, or we can choose those things which bring us happiness both now and forever.

CREATION OF MAN

Objective: To show that man must have been created, that he could not have evolved spontaneously.

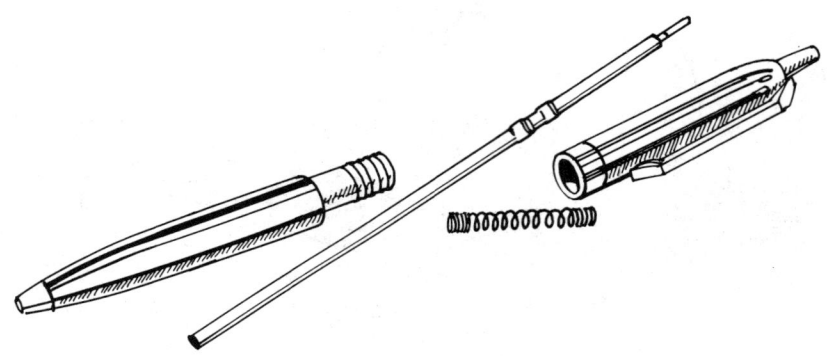

Material Needed:

1. Pen

Presentation:

1. Take the pen apart and show all the little parts that make it work.
2. Ask: Do you think that these parts could put themselves together to form a pen?

Lesson Application:

1. Our bodies, much more complicated than the pen, could not have been created by chance.
2. There must have been a creator, and he is our Heavenly Father.

DEATH

Objective: To show that we must constantly be prepared to meet God.

OBITUARIES

New York, New York—George Smith, died Saturday March 4, 1978 in New York at the age of 75.

Born July 30, 1902 in Albany, New York.

Denver, Colorado—Joyce Jones, 2 months, died May 3, 1979.
Born March 2, 1979 in Denver.

Material Needed:

1. Obituary column from the newspaper

Presentation:

1. Show the obituary column. Read one or two lines from several of the obituaries, showing that death comes to people of all ages.

Lesson Application:

1. We never know when the Lord is going to call us back to his presence. How many of us feel prepared to meet him today? We should set our priorities in life so that we are emphasizing that which is truly important.

DECEPTION

Objective: To show how Satan can deceive us.

Material Needed:

1. Two cookie jars: one filled with cookies to be eaten after the lesson—one filled with dirt or something undesirable

Presentation:

1. Show both cookie jars and ask someone what he would assume was in them.
2. Have two people come forward and each take one of the cookie jars. They should then look in the cookie jars without giving away the contents.
3. Have each of them take a turn telling the others how delicious the cookies in their jar look.
4. Have each class member choose the jar of cookies he wants.
5. Let them see what they have chosen.

Lesson Application:

1. The devil deceives us by making evil things look desirable. We therefore need to be very careful in our decisions.
2. Often Satan will try to deceive us with an idea that is a counterfeit of a true principle. He wants us to abuse good things—such as our ability to have children. We must constantly be on guard to know the real from the artificial.

Tools for Teaching 13

ENDURING TO THE END

Objective: To show how we can spiritually renew ourselves in order to endure to the end.

Material Needed:

1. A picture of a car being filled up with gas

Presentation:

1. Show the picture.

Lesson Application:

1. This car has run out of gas and is getting filled up to keep it moving.

2. As we go through life, we sometimes find ourselves running low on the spiritual energy necessary to face trials and temptations. We need to take time to renew ourselves and gain new strength. We can do this by pondering our blessings, studying the scriptures, and praying. This will give us the "fuel" we need to move toward eternal life.

ENTHUSIASM

Objective: To show the value of enthusiasm.

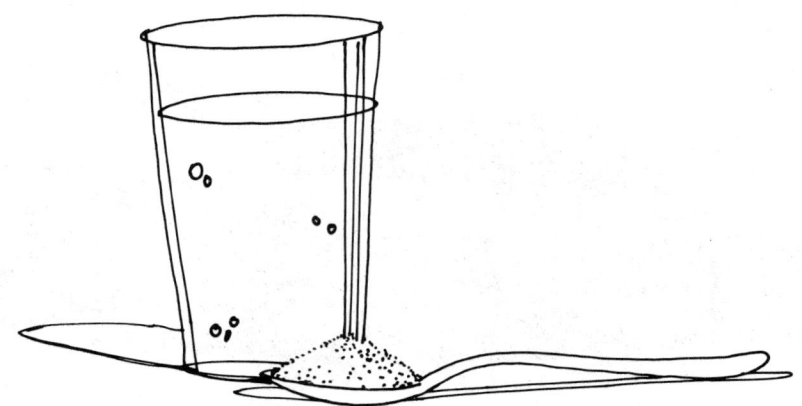

Material Needed:

1. A glass half filled with vinegar
2. A tablespoon of baking soda

Presentation:

1. Show the glass of vinegar.
2. Add the tablespoon of soda and watch the mixture fizz violently.

Lesson Application:

1. As long as we are unenthusiastic we are like the plain glass of vinegar. We can go through the motions of being active in the Church without really changing our own lives or helping others to change.
2. But true conversion and enthusiasm cause a great change within us. We will put a new spirit into our callings. We will tell others about the gospel.

Tools for Teaching 15

FAITH

Objective: To show that faith is important even though it is not tangible.

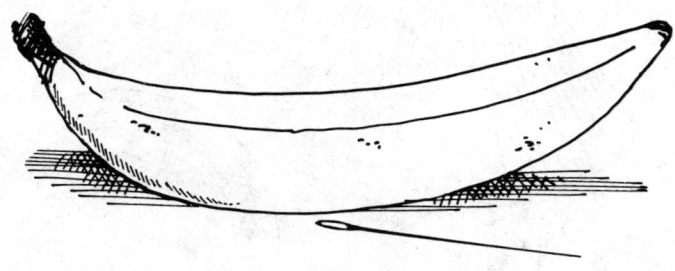

Material Needed:
1. One banana
2. Needle

Presentation:
1. Insert the needle through the skin of the banana. Then move it back and forth in such a manner as to cut the inside fruit into separate sections without creating any large holes in the peel. Repeat this process once more so that the fruit is severed into three sections without any noticeable break in the skin.
2. Ask the class if they believe that the banana is in three pieces inside the skin. Promise that the banana is in three pieces.
3. Then peel the banana and show the separate pieces to the class.

Lesson Application:
1. Something can be valuable even though it is not tangible. Some principles of the gospel are intangible and in apparent contradiction with man's knowledge; still, these principles are true and valuable.
2. Faith is not tangible, but it is of great value in our lives.
3. Just as we should have taken the word of the teacher of the lesson (who knew the truth), we should take the word of the living prophet who knows the truth today.

FAITH AND WORKS

Objective: To show that a combination of faith and works can help us reach our potential.

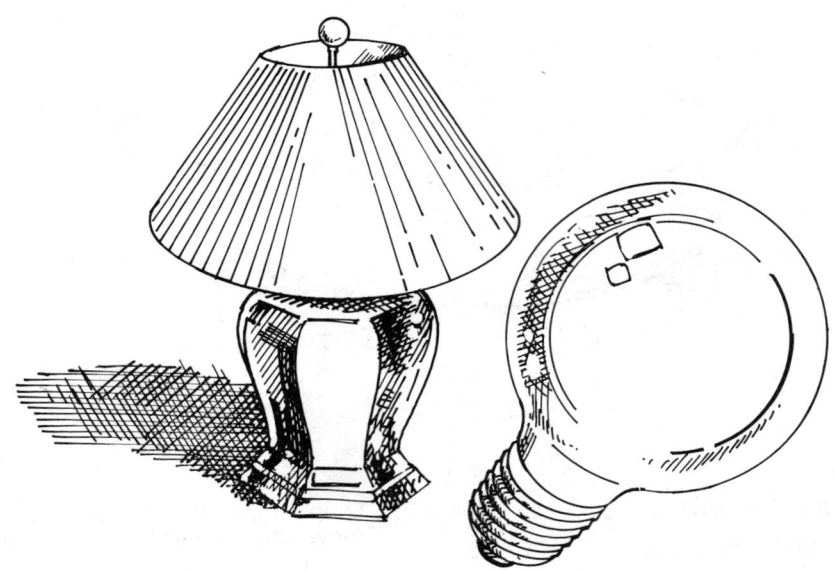

Material Needed:
1. Light bulb
2. Lamp (Both should be in working order)

Presentation:
1. Have a student hold the light bulb so the rest of the class can see it. Explain that the bulb is of little use at the present time but has potential.
2. Have another student turn on the lamp without a light bulb in it. Show that it also is of little use but has potential.
3. Have a student put the bulb in the lamp, plug it in, and turn it on.

Lesson Application:
1. We all have potential; we need to find our niche in life and get to work, otherwise our potential will be of little value.
2. Until we put the light bulb and the lamp together in the right way, they are of little use. So it is with faith and works. We must have both to fulfill our potential.

Tools for Teaching   17

FAMILY LOVE

Objective: To show that love is necessary to start and maintain a good family life.

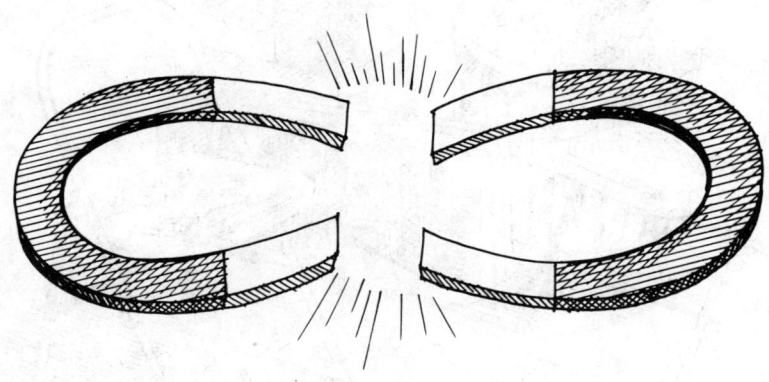

Material Needed:
1. Two magnets

Presentation:
1. Choose a married couple in the class and give them each a magnet. Have them explain how they met and came to love each other. Then have them put the two magnets together.
2. Then have them turn the magnets around so that they repel rather than attract each other.

Lesson Application:
1. Love brings two people together. After they are married they have children. Love unites the entire family.
2. Without this love the family will lack strength and may fall apart. We need to take the proper steps to keep it strong.

FORGIVING OURSELVES

Objective: To show the need to forgive ourselves.

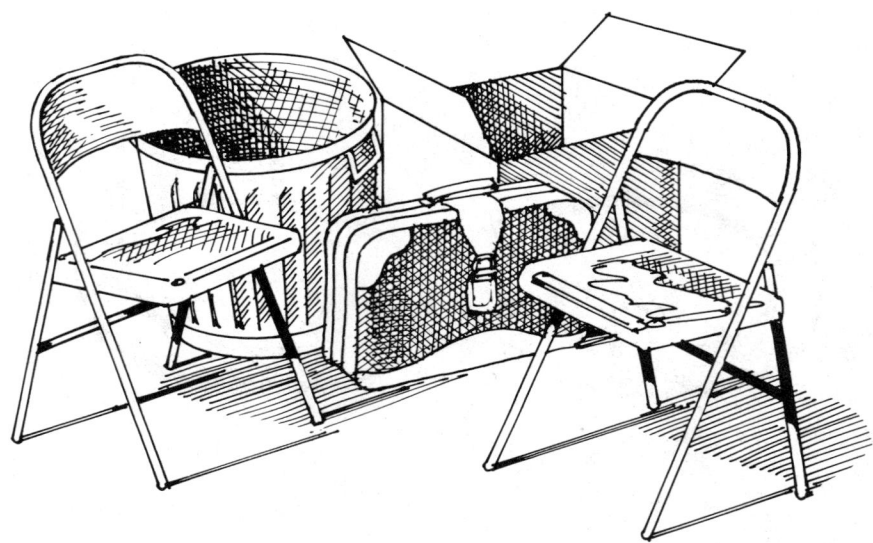

Material Needed:

1. Chairs and other large objects

Presentation:

1. Create a maze with chairs and other objects. Have a volunteer shut his eyes and try to go through the maze backwards. He will undoubtedly move very slowly, making many mistakes.

2. When he has made it through the maze, have him walk through it again, this time with his eyes open and walking forward. He will have no problem walking through it quickly and easily.

Lesson Application:

1. When we fail to forgive ourselves, we are, in a sense, walking backwards with our eyes closed, glued to the things of the past and insensitive to the things of the future. We are neither accurate, effective, nor quick to accomplish things.

2. We need to learn from experience and try not to repeat our mistakes, but needlessly punishing ourselves will only create further problems.

GOALS

Objective: To show the importance of setting goals and working to accomplish them.

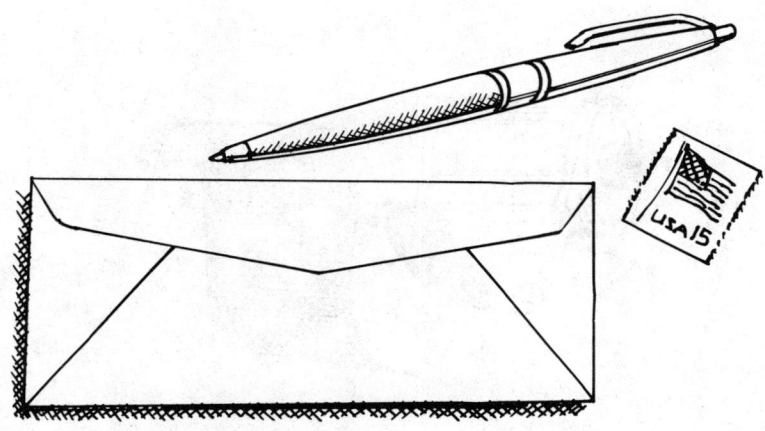

Material Needed:

1. A sealed envelope with a letter inside
2. A stamp
3. A pen

Presentation:

1. Show the sealed envelope and explain that it contains an important letter.
2. Write an address on the envelope.
3. Place a stamp on the envelope.

Lesson Application:

1. If we don't have goals, we are like the blank envelope—we have no direction.
2. Setting goals is like putting an address on the envelope: we know where we want to go in life. (Our main goal should be to reach the celestial kingdom.)
3. The stamp is like the price we have to pay to accomplish our goal—this means sacrificing, keeping the commandments, serving others, and doing all we can to reach our goals.

GOSPEL

Objective: To show that mere exposure to the gospel is not enough.

Material Needed:
1. Exposed roll of film

Presentation:
1. Show the film.

Lesson Application:
1. Just as this roll of film has been exposed to the light, we Latter-day Saints have been exposed to the gospel. We have Christ's example to follow. But if we do not develop ourselves, our exposure is of no use to us or anyone else. We need to develop ourselves so that other people will see our testimonies and want to follow our examples.

GOSPEL ENRICHMENT

Objective: To show how the gospel can enrich our lives.

Material Needed:

1. Blender
2. Ice cream
3. Milk

Presentation:

1. Pour some milk into the blender.
2. Add a little ice cream.
3. Have the class observe that the milk shake is not very desirable if it is not mixed.
4. Have them also observe that if too little ice cream is added the milk shake will still not be desirable.

Lesson Application:

1. Mixing a healthy portion of ice cream with the milk is like incorporating gospel principles into our everyday lives. Our lives become richer and much more fulfilling.
2. The gospel gives substance to our lives. It helps us find meaning and direction. The more gospel we have in our lives, the better.

HARDSHIPS

Objective: To encourage class members to bear hardships without complaining.

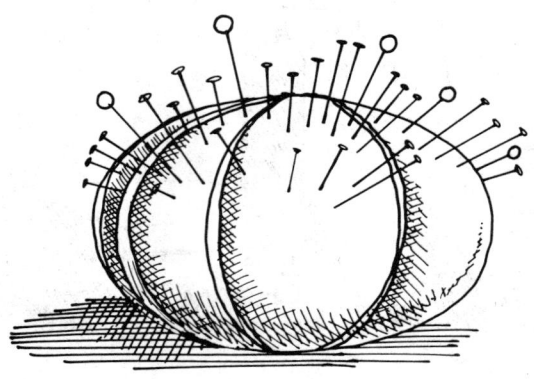

Material Needed:

1. Pin cushion
2. Pins

Presentation:

1. Stick a few pins into the pin cushion.

Lesson Application:

1. Pretend you are this pin cushion. What do you do as I stick pins into you? In life, we often get "stuck" with a trying experience or a difficult assignment. Sometimes we find ourselves complaining or asking "Why me?"

2. The pin cushion bears its hardships almost unknowingly. When the pin is pulled out, there is no trace of where it went in. And on some special pin cushions, the pin is sharpened when it is pulled out.

3. If we learn to bear hardships without complaining, they will strengthen us.

HEART OF GOLD

Objective: To show that beauty is discovered not with the eye but with the heart.

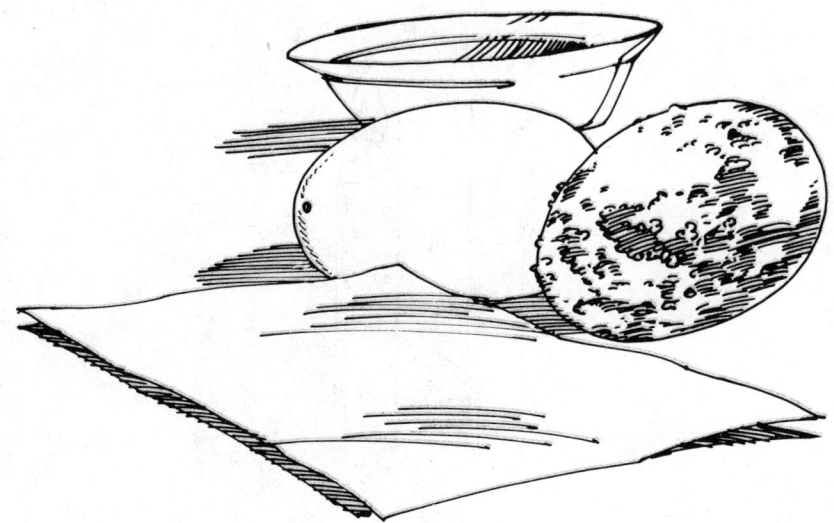

Material Needed:

1. Two raw eggs
2. One bowl
3. Paper towel

Presentation:

1. Before class, make pinholes in both ends of one egg. Blow out the yolk and white and allow the inside of the egg to dry. Roll the other egg in dirt or grease so that it appears quite undesirable.
2. In class, hold up both eggs and ask which one the class members would like to eat. (They will select the hollow egg.)
3. After the selection is made crush the clean shell in your hand, revealing its hollowness.
4. Follow this up by cracking the dirty egg into the bowl, revealing a "heart of gold."

Lesson Application:

1. We should not judge others by outward appearances; it can often be misleading. It is important to look for the "heart of gold" in everyone.

LIGHT

Objective: To show that our testimonies must be strong.

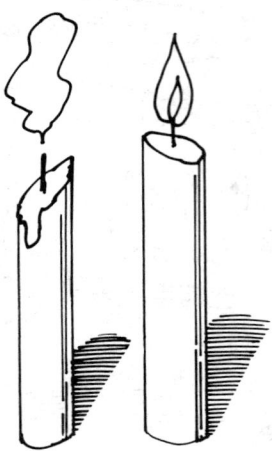

Material Needed:

1. Two candles (One should be a trick candle that will relight after it is blown out)
2. Matches

Presentation:

1. Light both candles. Then blow them out. (The trick candle will relight.)

Lesson Application:

1. If our testimonies are not strong, they will be blown out by the winds of adversity. But if we strengthen our testimonies through prayer and righteous living, we will be able to stay true to the Lord despite trials and difficulties.

Tools for Teaching 25

MARRIAGE

Objective: To show the need for unity in marriage.

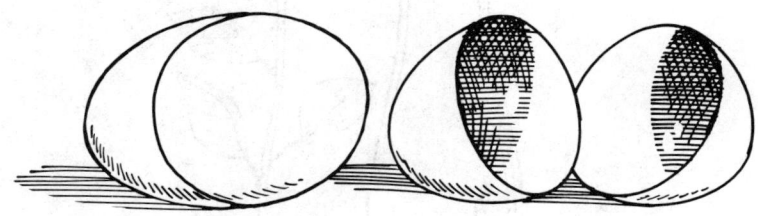

Material Needed:
1. Plastic egg
2. Table

Presentation:
1. Take the egg apart and attempt to roll the two halves across the table. (They will not roll because of their shape.)
2. Put the halves together. Show how they roll smoothly across the table.

Lesson Application:
1. If two people are truly united, they can move together toward eternal life.

26 Tools for Teaching

MORAL CLEANLINESS

Objective: To show the importance of keeping ourselves morally clean.

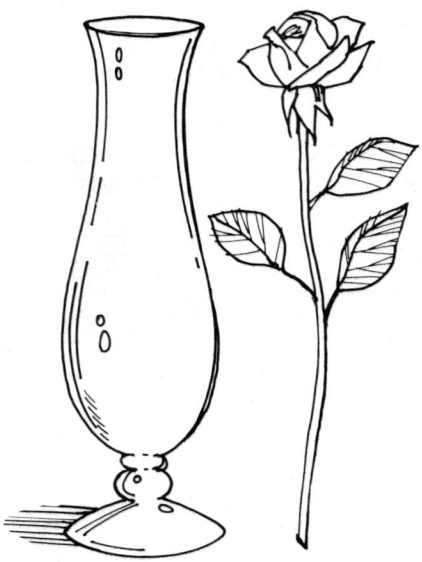

Material Needed:

1. A beautiful budding rose
2. A vase

Presentation:

1. While displaying the rose in the vase, talk of its beauty. Bring out the fact that it is just beginning to bloom and expand its beauty. Then take the rose out of the vase and begin breaking off petals and bending the stem.

Lesson Application:

1. Like the rose, our bodies are initially beautiful and pure. However, if we violate the law of chastity we lose that beauty and purity. Just as we would take care of a beautiful rose, let us keep ourselves morally clean.

OBSTACLES

Objective: To show that the Lord gives us obstacles to help us grow stronger.

Material Needed:

1. A round, smooth stone

Presentation:

1. Pass the stone around and allow class members to examine it.

Lesson Application:

1. A stone like this becomes round and smooth by rolling down a river or stream. Its rough edges are worn away as it rubs against other stones. This rough treatment seems as if it would damage the stone, but it actually polishes the stone and makes it more beautiful.

2. As we go through life we encounter problems and tribulations that may seem at the time to be hurting us. But it is by meeting and overcoming obstacles that we become stronger.

OUR BODIES

Objective: To show that our bodies are temples of God.

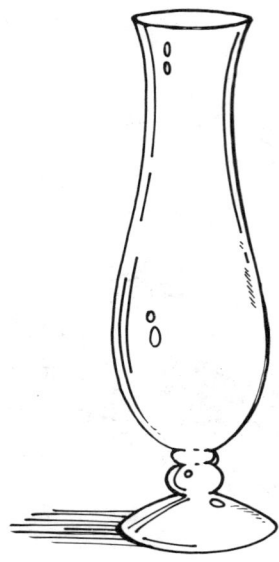

Material Needed:

1. White flower vase

Presentation:

1. Show the vase.

Lesson Application:

1. The vase is relatively pretty, but serves no purpose unless it holds flowers. And to garnish it you add ferns, leaves, and ribbon.

2. Like the vase, our bodies serve no useful purpose unless we use them to fulfill their true purpose—service to God.

3. We should be much more concerned with our bodies than we are with objects of the world because our bodies are the temples of God.

Tools for Teaching   29

OVERCOMING PROBLEMS

Objective: To show that by staying well rounded in all aspects of life, we can bounce back easily when problems arise.

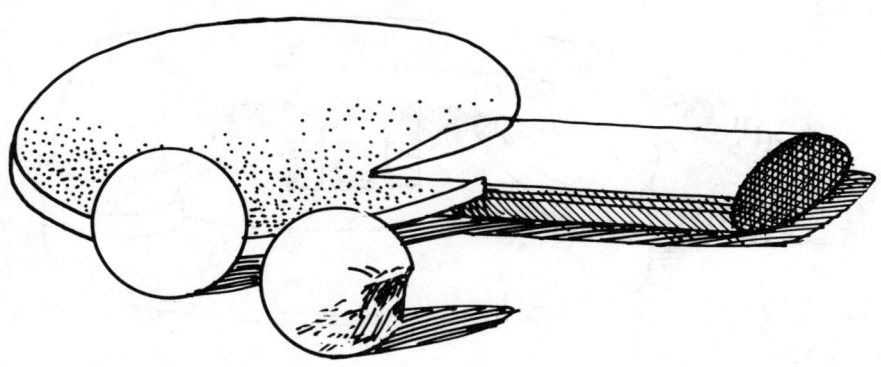

Material Needed:
1. Two Ping-Pong balls (one in good shape and one that is dented so that it will not bounce straight)
2. A Ping-Pong paddle

Presentation:
1. Drop the bad ball and tap it with the paddle. It will not bounce correctly.
2. Now do the same with the good ball; it will bounce right back up.

Lesson Application:
1. The paddle represents problems and challenges that we are faced with each day.
2. If we stay well rounded in all aspects of life, we will be able to bounce back when we are confronted with problems.

PRAYER

Objective: To show that we must make a genuine effort to communicate with the Lord.

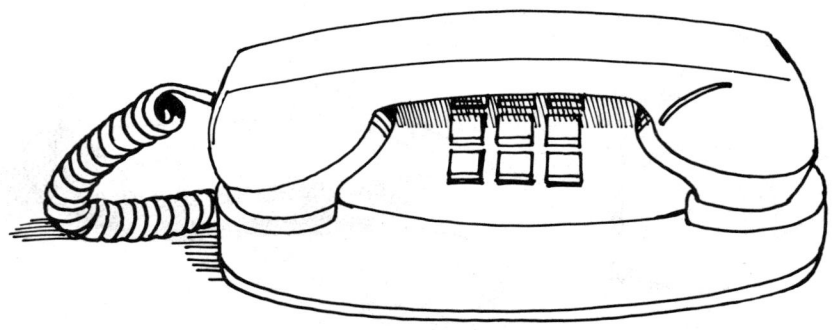

Material Needed:

1. Toy telephone

Presentation:

1. Show telephone. Say: "If you wanted to talk to a good friend about a problem, would you look at the phone and wish your friend would call? If you did that, you might never hear from your friend, and you would have to keep all your problems to yourself. What would you do? Why, you would dial his number and wait while it rang so he would have time to answer the phone. You would be patient and not slam the phone down just as he answered. After all, he is your friend and you need to speak to him.

Lesson Application:

1. This is something like talking to our Heavenly Father. His line is never busy. He loves you more than any friend. You need to speak to him and let him know of your problems. You must make the first effort and be patient on your knees. Do not be the cause of a communication gap. Make sure your phone is in order, then express yourself, and listen for an answer.

PRAYER

Objective: To show why we should pray more than once a day.

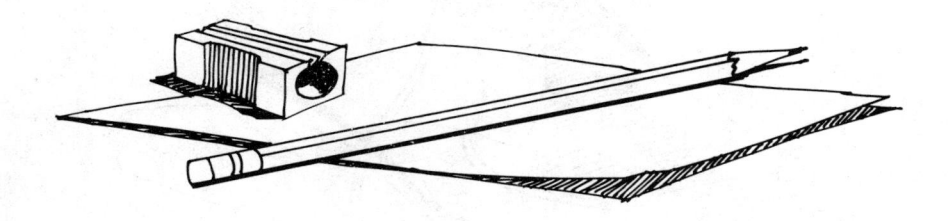

Material Needed:

1. Pencil
2. Pencil sharpener
3. Paper

Presentation:

1. Ask one person to sharpen the pencil.
2. Ask someone to write with this sharpened pencil. Note how well it writes.
3. Have someone write a lot with the pencil or even scribble to wear down the point. Note how the marks it now makes are less fine and clear.
4. Ask someone to sharpen the pencil and write with it again. Note how well it works.

Lesson Application:

1. When we have morning prayer it is like sharpening ourselves. We then can write more clearly on our life's record. But as we go through the day, things wear on us and make us dull. We need to pray or keep sharpening ourselves so that we make a clear imprint on life.
2. Repentance sharpens us and sin dulls us.
3. To live righteously we need to pray often.

PRIESTHOOD

Objective: To demonstrate the binding power of the priesthood.

Material Needed:

1. One shoe with a shoelace

Presentation:

1. Put the shoe on without the shoelace and walk around. Then show how much better the shoe fits when it is laced and tied.

Lesson Application:

1. The priesthood is the binding force in the family and the Church. Just as the lace enables us to walk more easily, the priesthood helps us to function effectively at home and at Church. The priesthood gives us direction and order.

Tools for Teaching 33

PRINCIPLES OF THE GOSPEL

Objective: To show that the different principles of the gospel all fit together.

Material Needed:

1. Orange

Presentation:

1. Show the class the orange. Tell them how good it is. Note its shape and color.
2. Peel the orange, showing the different sections.

Lesson Application:

1. The orange is good from the outside in. The same is true with the gospel.
2. Just as the different sections of the orange fit together, the different principles of the gospel unite to form a perfect way of life. All of the principles are necessary.
3. We should share the gospel with others just as we would share a delicious orange.

PRINCIPLES AND ORDINANCES OF THE GOSPEL

Objective: To show the importance of having all four principles and ordinances.

Material Needed:

1. Chair with one leg detached

Presentation:

1. Have the class watch as you try to stand the chair on the floor or a table. It will tip over because one leg is missing.
2. Now attach the fourth leg so it is secure. Show the class that one can now sit in the chair.

Lesson Application:

1. The first four principles and ordinances of the gospel are faith, repentance, baptism, and the laying on of hands for the gift of the Holy Ghost. A person cannot be secure in the gospel if one of these is missing.
2. When a person has faith, repents, is baptized, and receives the Holy Ghost, he is fully prepared to overcome his past mistakes and dedicate himself to the service of the Lord.

PRIORITIES

Objective: To show that we can use the gospel to set priorities.

Material Needed:

1. A yellow felt-tip pen
2. A marked book

Presentation:

1. Show the pen to the class and a page from the book that has been marked. Explain that you use the marker to emphasize important passages. This helps you to recognize essential points when you review for a test.

Lesson Application:

1. In our everyday lives many things demand our time and attention. The gospel gives us the perspective we need to emphasize those things which are truly important. If we use the gospel to set priorities, we will be able to pass the "test" of this mortal existence.

PROCRASTINATION

Objective: To show the futility of procrastination.

Material Needed:
1. Two glasses (one with water, the other empty)

Presentation:
1. Hold up the empty glass. Ask the class what an empty glass is good for.
2. Pour water into the empty glass. Now ask what value it has.

Lesson Application:
1. If we procrastinate or wait for things to happen, our lives will be empty, like the glass.
2. We can't just sit by and wait for things to happen. We need to take action and fill our lives with meaningful activities.

PROTECTION

Objective: To show that we need to keep the commandments in order to have the Lord's protection and guidance.

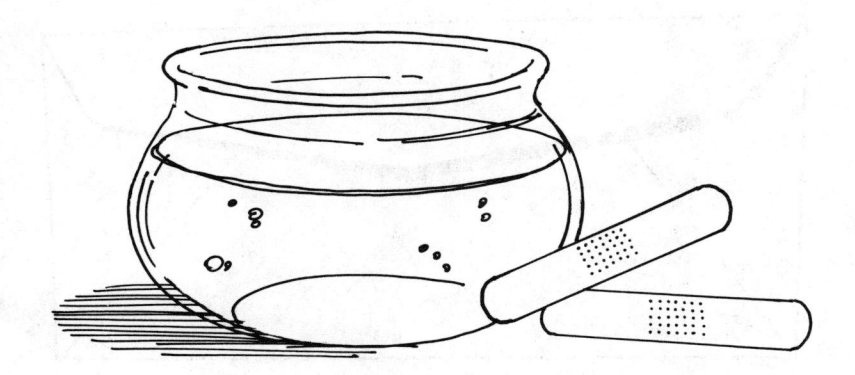

Material Needed:
1. Bowl of water
2. Two Band-Aids

Presentation:
1. Ask for a volunteer and have him dunk one hand in the bowl of water.
2. Put a Band-Aid on the back of each of his hands. (The Band-Aid on the dry hand will stick, but the one on the wet hand will not.)

Lesson Application:
1. If we make ourselves unclean (wet) by sinning, we will not have the Spirit of the Lord with us.
2. But if we keep the commandments and stay clean (dry), we will have the Lord's protection and his guidance.

PURPOSE IN LIFE

Objective: To show the importance of having purpose in our lives.

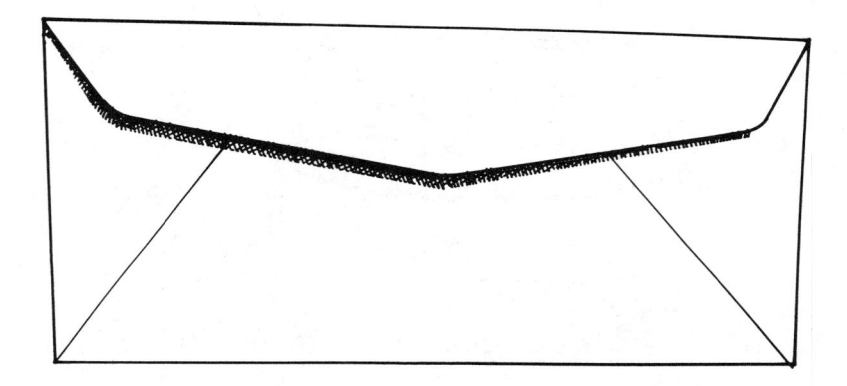

Material Needed:
1. A plain white envelope

Presentation:
1. Show the envelope. Explain how it has nothing in it or on it and is therefore not important to anyone. It fulfills no significant purpose.
2. If something important (such as a letter) is put inside the envelope, it becomes valuable.

Lesson Application:
1. Some people, like plain white envelopes, are merely existing—they have no purpose in life. The gospel can help all of us fill our lives with meaning; life will thus become exciting and challenging.

READINESS

Objective: To show that unless we are prepared we will not be able to fulfill our purpose.

Material Needed:
1. Two electric irons (one hot, one cold)
2. One wrinkled cloth

Presentation:
1. Attempt to iron the wrinkled cloth with the cold iron.
2. Press wrinkled cloth with the hot iron.

Lesson Application:
1. If we are unprepared we cannot perform our duties effectively.
2. If we have spent the time necessary to prepare, we will be able to fulfill our true purpose in life.
3. We must prepare and stay close to the proper source of power—the Lord.

REPENTANCE

Objective: To show the importance of repentance.

Material Needed:

1. A book of remembrance
2. A pencil with an eraser on it

Presentation:

1. Show the pencil and the book of remembrance.

Lesson Application:

1. Each of us has the opportunity to write our life story. Our Father in heaven knew that we would make some mistakes, that is why we have an eraser on our pencil—the principle of repentance—to wipe away our mistakes.
2. When we present our life history to the Great Judge, he will not ask about the things that have been erased.
3. We can serve the Lord and our fellowmen better after we have repented.

SATAN

Objective: To demonstrate the reality of Satan's power.

Material Needed:

1. Candle
2. Paper trough
3. Vinegar
4. Soda
5. Glass
6. Matches

Presentation:

1. Light the candle. Make a paper trough. Mix vinegar and soda in the glass. (The vinegar and soda make an invisible gas.)
2. Pour this gas down to the flame. The flame will go out.

Lesson Application:

1. Satan is real even though we cannot see him. He has the power to smother and kill us with his ideas and ways just as the gas has the ability to smother and kill the flame. The flame represents our souls and the gas represents the invisible power of Satan.
2. We need to stay close to the Lord so that he will protect our flames and keep them burning.

SELF-ESTEEM

Objective: To show that building up one's ego is good, but that inflating it too much is harmful.

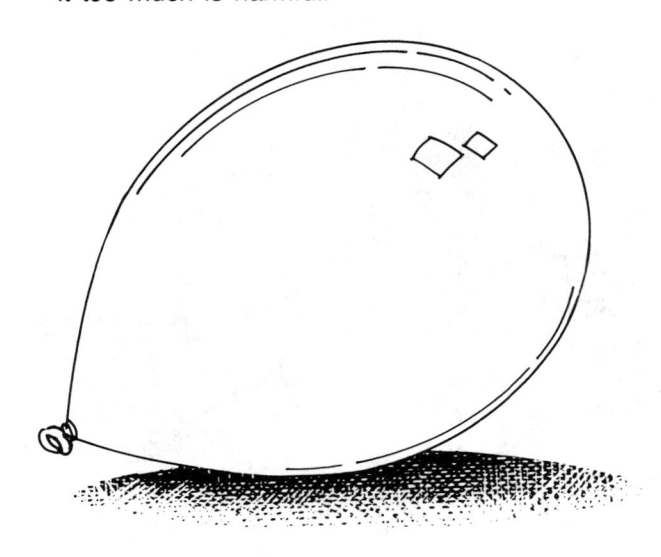

Material Needed:

1. Balloon

Presentation:

1. Show the balloon before it is blown up. Tell the class the balloon is not worth much if it is not blown up.
2. Blow up the balloon. Tell how it can now be used as a toy.
3. Continue to blow up the balloon until it pops. Tell how it is worthless again.

Lesson Application:

1. We are not very valuable if we have no self-esteem.
2. We become valuable as we accomplish things and discover our own good qualities.
3. We lose our value if we become too concerned with ourselves and get caught up in pride.

Tools for Teaching 43

SERVICE

Objective: To show how negative actions can affect our ability to serve.

Material Needed:

1. Ten blocks

Presentation:

1. Before class, write the name of a negative action on each block. Examples are gossip, hate, and jealousy.
2. In class, briefly discuss each of the ten negative actions. As you do so, stack the bricks in a wall.

Lesson Application:

1. We must rid ourselves of these qualities so that we do not build a barrier between us and those we need to serve.

SIN

Objective: To show that it takes time and effort to overcome sin.

Material Needed:

1. Small jar
2. Container of water labeled "Sin"
3. Container of vegetable oil labeled "Clean living"

Presentation:

1. Pour some vegetable oil into the jar and show the class how even and consistent it looks.
2. Pour the same amount of water into the jar.
3. Shake the jar to show the class how the water affects the oil.
4. Let the jar sit while the water and oil separate.

Lesson Application:

1. We are originally pure like the oil.
2. When we sin, however, our lives are polluted.
3. The separation of the oil and water represents repentance. Note that this takes time and effort.

SPEAKING KIND WORDS

Objective: To show the importance of speaking kind words to others.

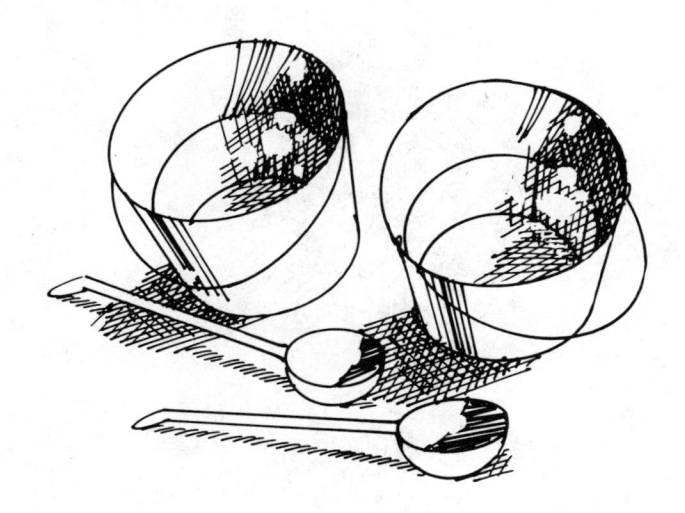

Material Needed:
1. Two small buckets half filled with water
2. Two dippers

Presentation:
1. Have two people come to the front of the room. Give them each a bucket of water and a dipper.
2. Have them converse. When person number one says something kind to person number two he should take water from his own bucket and put it in person number two's bucket. When person number one says something unkind, he should take water from number two's bucket and put it in his own. Have person number two do the same.

Lesson Application:
1. We are always—through our conversation—adding to or taking away from the lives of others. We should remember how much good kind words can do.

SPIRITUALITY

Objective: To show that we should not separate ourselves from our source of spiritual strength—the Lord.

Material Needed:

1. A dry leaf
2. A living plant

Presentation:

1. Show the dry leaf and ask why it dried up. (Answer: Because it has been separated from its source of life—the plant or tree.)
2. Show the living plant. Ask why the leaves are still green. (Answer: Because they are still attached to the plant.)

Lesson Application:

1. If we separate ourselves from the source of our spiritual strength—the Lord—we will suffer spiritual death.
2. We can keep close to the Lord and stay alive spiritually by praying regularly, reading the scriptures, attending church, and following the prophet.

STRONG PHYSICAL BODY

Objective: To show the effects of taking care of our bodies.

Material Needed:

1. One pair of boots (One boot should be highly shined with a clean, new lace. The other should be dirty and water marked, with a worn lace.)

Presentation:

1. Show the class the boots and explain that the boots have always been worn at the same time.
2. Ask why the two boots are so different now. (The difference lies in how the boots were treated after they were worn.)

Lesson Application:

1. Each of us goes through difficult physical experiences, such as hard work and illness, but even when we have similar experiences we do not recover equally.
2. Our bodies are the temples of God. We should take care of ourselves and keep close to the Lord (the creator of our bodies) so that he will bless us with physical strength.

TALENTS

Objective: To show that it is not what we are given, but what we do with what we are given that determines our success in this life.

Material Needed:

1. Clear bowl
2. Water
3. Several balls of clay of various sizes

Presentation:

1. Show how the different balls of clay can be molded into many different shapes.
2. Show that one piece of clay will float if molded like a boat.
3. Show that every piece of clay can be molded to float.

Lesson Application:

1. We all have different talents, and we can mold our lives many different ways.
2. But regardless of the number of talents we have, we can all mold our lives so that we do not sink or fail.

TALENTS

Objective: To show that the talents of each family member are needed to make the family a complete unit.

Material Needed:
1. Ball of string
2. Scissors

Presentation:
1. Select four or five class members to come forward. Give them the ball of string and have each person cut off a section of string.
2. Then have each person describe the talents of the person on his right. These two people should then tie their pieces of string together; eventually a circle will be formed.

Lesson Application:
1. Just as each piece of string was necessary to form the circle, the talents of each family member are needed to unite the family. We can strengthen the family unit by complimenting others on their talents.

TESTIMONY

Objective: To show how we need to have a strong testimony.

Material Needed:

1. Fan
2. Rock
3. Feather

Presentation:

1. Hold the feather in front of the fan, and show how it blows away. Hold the rock in front of the fan.

Lesson Application:

1. If our testimonies are weak, we will be caught up in the whirlwinds of the world.
2. But if they are strong and have their foundations in Christ, we will be able to stand firm despite trials and temptations.

TESTIMONY

Objective: To show that a testimony has to be strong and durable and needs to be polished.

Material Needed:

1. Small ceramic or glass object
2. Rock

Presentation:

1. Show the ceramic object and the rock to the class.
2. Note the differences between the two.
3. Drop the glass piece. Drop the rock.
4. Discuss the outcome of the drop.
5. Explain that while the ceramic object is very beautiful to look at, it is delicate and will shatter when dropped. The rock is not necessarily beautiful but it is strong and durable and may not be damaged at all when it is dropped. (If it is, the nick can easily be smoothed out.) We can continually polish a rock and make it more beautiful every day.

Lesson Application:

1. Our testimonies must be strong and durable or they will be broken by temptation and difficult experiences.
2. We should continually "polish" our testimonies by doing such things as praying and going to church.

TIME

Objective: To show that our time is limited here on earth.

Material Needed:

1. An alarm clock

Presentation:

1. Set the alarm so that it will go off while you are teaching the lesson.

Lesson Application:

1. After the alarm goes off, say the following: Just as we did not know when the alarm would go off, we do not know how long we will be on earth. We should strive to do the right things today.

Tools for Teaching   53

TRUST

Objective: To encourage us to trust in the Lord.

Material Needed:
1. A blindfold
2. An obstacle course

Presentation:
1. Select two members of the class who are good friends. Have one of them put on a blindfold. His friend should then help him through the obstacle course. The blindfolded person may consult his friend for suggestions and advice, but he must make the final decisions.

Lesson Application:
1. The Lord is our best friend. We are, in a sense, blindfolded as we travel down life's path. We may pray to him for help, but we must make the final decisions. The Lord will not lead us astray (just as the blindfolded person's friend would not lead him astray).

TRUST

Objective: To emphasize the importance of having complete trust in the Lord.

Material Needed:

1. Glass or jar
2. Spoon
3. Seed
4. Dark cookie crumbs

Presentation:

1. Ask someone to come and plant the seed in this good potting soil (cookie crumbs). Have the person use the spoon to make a hole and place the seed in the hole. Now, before he covers the seed up, ask him to eat a spoonful of soil. Promise him that he will like it. If he trusts you, he will eat it and will discover it is not soil at all but cookie crumbs.

Lesson Application:

1. Many times during our lives we must rely on faith instead of going by what we can clearly see before us. Yet, we should trust in our Heavenly Father, for he will never lead us astray.

UNITY

Objective: To show the need for unity among ward members.

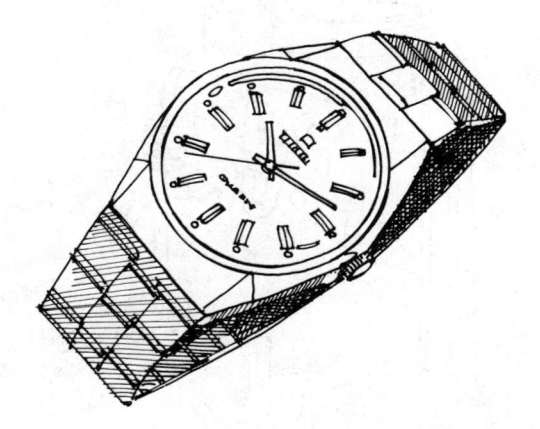

Material Needed:

1. Wrist watch

Presentation:

1. Show the watch to the class members and let them pass it around so they can see that it works and shows the correct time.

Lesson Application:

1. All of the parts of the watch must be in good working order to enable it to run efficiently. One part of the watch that is not in good condition can have harmful effects on other parts and thus cause the watch itself to function improperly. To prevent needless wear, one should have the watch cleaned, oiled, and checked periodically.

2. So it is with the members of a ward or branch. When one member fails to serve to the best of his ability, another member has to either prod the first to do better or follow behind, doing the things the first did not do. And thus the performances of a few individuals can affect the entire ward.

3. Just as the watch must be checked and cleaned periodically, ward members must often evaluate their progress and see how they can improve. Through interviews, self-evaluation, and goal setting ward members can work together effectively.

USE OF TIME

Objective: To show that we have more time than we think.

Material Needed:

1. Jar labeled "24 Hours"
2. Small objects such as marbles and blocks
3. Salt

Presentation:

1. Put objects into jar until the jar is full. When jar is full, pour salt into jar until all the cracks are full.

Lesson Application:

1. We all have twenty-four hours a day. The objects stand for parts of our life which take up time: sleep, study, work, meals, classes, social life, etc. The salt represents all that we can do if we use the free minutes we have and budget our time wisely.

WELL-ROUNDED PERSON

Objective: To show that a well-rounded person is a stronger person.

Material Needed:

1. Two eggs
2. A bowl

Presentation:

1. Have someone come forward and show how easy it is to break an egg by squeezing it with his fingers.
2. Now give that person the other egg and have him hold it lengthwise in the palm of his hand. Challenge him to break the egg by squeezing his hand. (He cannot do it.)

Lesson Application:

1. Since the fibers of an egg run from end to end, it cannot be broken when held in a certain way. We can, however, easily break an egg if we know its weak areas.
2. Satan tempts us by working on our weaknesses. We need to be strong all over so that no amount of pressure will make us yield.

THE WHOLE ARMOR OF GOD

Objective: To show how putting on the "whole armor of God" protects us from "the fiery darts of the wicked."

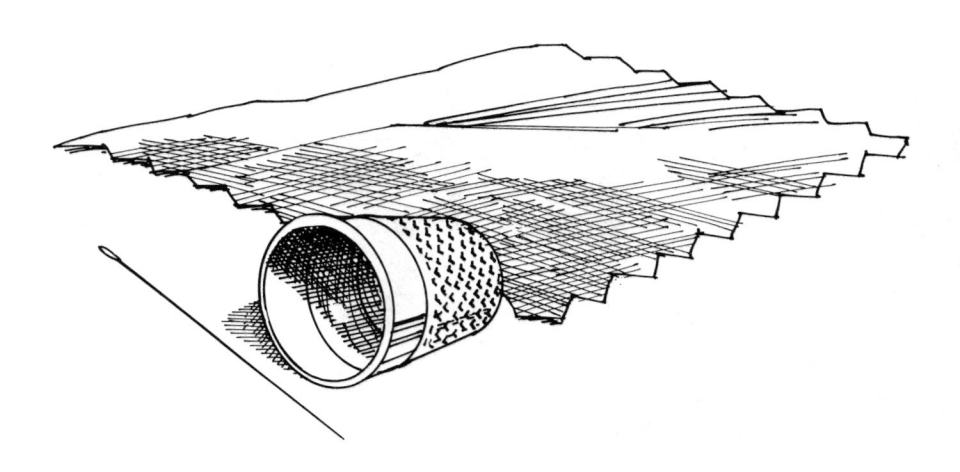

Material Needed:

1. Thimble
2. Needle
3. Piece of fabric

Presentation:

1. Put the thimble on your finger.
2. Explain how it protects you from the prick of the needle.
3. Demonstrate its effectiveness by using it to push a needle into a piece of fabric.

Lesson Application:

1. This thimble protects us from the prick of the needle and saves us from unnecessary pain. The same is true with the armor of God. If we put on the whole armor, we are protected from the fiery darts of the wicked, and are spared needless pain.
2. See D&C 27:15-18 for further discussion.